A Scar Upon Our Voice

MARY BURRITT CHRISTIANSEN POETRY SERIES
V. B. PRICE, SERIES EDITOR

Also available in the University of New Mexico Press
Mary Burritt Christiansen Poetry Series

Miracles of Sainted Earth
Victoria Edwards Tester

Poets of the Non-Existent City
edited by Estelle Gershgoren Novak

Selected Poems of Gabriela Mistral
edited by Ursula K. Le Guin

Deeply Dug In
R. L. Barth

Amulet Songs: Poems Selected and New
Lucile Adler

In Company: An Anthology of New Mexico Poets
edited by Lee Bartlett, V. B. Price, and Dianne Edenfield Edwards

Tiempos Lejanos
Nasario García

Refuge of Whirling Light: Poems
Mary Beath

Mary Burritt
Christiansen
Poetry Series

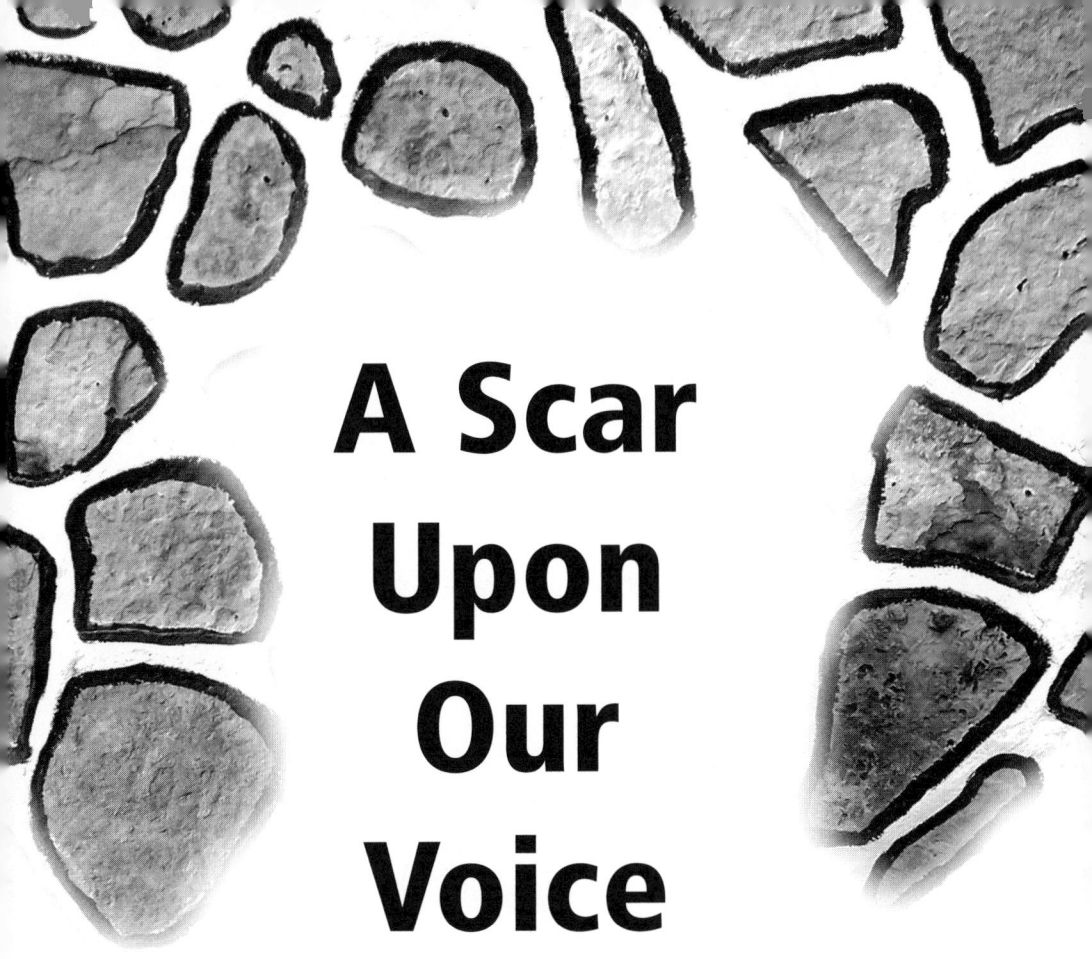

A Scar
Upon
Our
Voice

Robin Coffee

University of New Mexico Press

Albuquerque

Library of Congress Cataloging-in-Publication Data

Coffee, Robin, 1953–
A scar upon our voice / Robin Coffee.
p. cm. — (Mary Burritt Christiansen poetry series)
ISBN 0-8263-3629-9 (alk. paper)
1. Indians of North America—Poetry.
I. Title. II. Series.
PS3603.O315S28 2005
811'.6—dc22

2005012478

DESIGN AND COMPOSITION: *Mina Yamashita*

To my daughter,

Crystal Amy Dawn Coffee

and to

my Mother

Special thanks to

Kelly Denise Vann

Contents

Existential Warrior (2003)

Foreword

Robin Coffee is a Native American poet who found his own path through the desolation of colonialism and the never ending shadows of genocide. As he writes in his preface, "I was lost for a long time. I had discovered that my government wanted to terminate all tribes. . . . My government was responsible for my lack of tribal traditions, my loss of a tribal tongue, my loss of tribal identity, and my perception that my culture was almost dead and was surely going to die. I was made to feel ashamed for wanting to be Indian."

A Cherokee/Creek/Yankton Sioux, Coffee lives in Tahlequah, Okalahoma. He was the 2000 winner of the Cherokee Historical Society's Cherokee Medal of Honor for his work as a poet and writer and for the inspiration he's brought to Native American young people over many years.

The poems in *A Scar Upon Our Voice* have a deep heartedness, a generosity of spirit, and a wise compassion that make them what I like to call "a hand in the dark" for people in trouble, or for youngsters, or anyone struggling for growth and maturity. They are poems of inner strength, spiritual opening, and ethical clarity. They speak to all people who find themselves in situations of diffuse or overt oppression, who've been kept back by custom or malice, unable to break through the great barriers of prejudice, poverty, and exploitation. In his poem "Anti-System Indian," he says,

Compromise is a betrayal
Killer of spirit
A conflict of the heart
Walking the path of the system
Takes me away
From who I am
It takes strong drink
To numb the spirit
Of a heart
That wants to live
But cannot find a reason why

Sleepless nights of anger
Searching desperately
Never finding
The voice of the lost. . . .

Through years of struggle, Robin Coffee found his own path by "a simple gesture born out of kindness," the gift of his voice to others in need. In the title poem of this book that Coffee wrote for his mother, he says,

We have never spoken
To each other
In our native tongue
We speak
A foreign language
Like
A scar upon our voice. . . .

Every time we speak
We hear this battle wound

Our words
Have blood upon them
So we cherish
The silence between us. . . .
You have taught me
To speak
In another voice. . . .

Unlike so many works in the past associated with Native Americans, *A Scar Upon Our Voice* is not a translation, not a well-meaning but distant offering of an anthropologist honoring a folk tradition. Robin Coffee speaks in the first person, in a foreign but first language, directly from his own experience, and from a position of spiritual calm and moral power. The anger here is the anger of a person who does not believe the propaganda that makes it seem better to be white than Indian, as Conroy Chino, an investigative reporter in New Mexico, recently said on PBS. Coffee refuses to submit to false and demeaning stereotypes, or to anything that deprives anyone, for that matter, of their inherent rights as a human being. He writes, "The founding fathers/Set into motion/through acts of legislation/The method of my death/A slow beating. . . ." In the poem "Endless Void," he says of despair that "When living seems wrong/And/Dying right/It's like walking dead/Into/An endless night. . . ." But in the poem "Prayer" he affirms the freedom of courage: "With a gentle hand/Comfort me/Give me strength/To walk/In my own/Silent resistence."

UNM Press and the Mary Burritt Christiansen Poetry Series are proud to publish this book of poems written over many decades to both express and to model for young people what it's like to reveal to the world inner truths and sufferings and, most of all, the overcomings that so often arise from deep and brave honesty. This unique and important book will have, I think, a wide and devoted audience all across Indian Country and beyond for many years because it gives voice to not only the secret pain of Native Americans, but of all people oppressed or swept aside by greed, malice, and power madness of others.

—V. B. Price
Albuquerque, May 2005

Preface

I drove out to Cherokee Landing today to visit a place I haven't been to in many years. I came out here to clear my mind, quiet the noise of my life, to visit the water and the wind, to walk the rocky shoreline, and to become part of the death-like appearance of the grass and trees. I find hope in knowing that in a few weeks the silent signal will awaken the grass and the trees will begin to show their buds of life. I came that my heart will see more clearly and I can reach out with greater understanding. I saw my niece and her daughter Naomi today as I was driving here. I was stopped at a red light and they honked. Naomi had her beautiful face out the window and she waved and called my name as they drove past. Her face was full of the excitement of just being alive. Her eyes were full of innocence. I was glad to see them. As it is in my life, my gladness was touched with sadness.

I see our children so full of promise but as they become adolescents the innocence in their eyes is changed to a hardness and anger. The slowness of their smiles hints at a growing mistrust and I can see the almost invisible tracks of the tears that have been born out of betrayal and cried alone upon their faces. It is the silent turmoil that brings these tears and sets the youth on a journey without a path from which many are lost, forever.

I was lost for a long time. I had discovered that my government wanted to terminate all tribes. My government had passed laws and allocated money to accomplish these misguided deeds. My government was responsible for my lack of tribal traditions, my loss of a tribal tongue, my loss of tribal identity, and my perception that my culture was almost dead and was surely going to die. I was made to feel ashamed for wanting to be Indian.

I was educated from the perspective of one culture but not from the perspective of my own culture. I was educated in this way all my life and had not known it. I did not know it because the truth was ever denied but because it was simply never spoken. The silence of my government and the silence of my educators enraged me, but the silence of my elders disheartened me. At the age when establishing an identity is the most important task, I became angry, rebellious, distrustful, and my heart turned away from this world.

It is betrayal when children are allowed to reach adolescence believing they belong to one culture and discovering that they actually belong to two cultures that are at odds with each other. Adolescence is a confusing and difficult period of change and natural development without the additional burden of having to choose which culture is yours or having to reconcile the two into an acceptable form of self-identity. The task is so difficult that many can never make a choice or can never reconcile the differences in the cultures. The betrayal of a system that raises children this way and the silence of a culture that allows the children to be raised this way is a burden that overwhelms adolescents in a critical time of their development. The feelings of anger, confusion, and mistrust born out of this betrayal can determine the paths of our children, forever. I stood at the crossroads of life with my shattered innocence and broken identity and felt alone. I could see no path that would lead me to a place where I would feel I belonged. The system encouraged me to continue on its assembly line process of producing citizens. The anger in my heart encouraged me to resist the system because it led to betrayal. I had no Indian culture to wrap its arms around me, comfort and guide me, or to lead me into the future. I could see that if you killed the Indianness of me there would be no man to save. I could not choose to remain quiet and follow the path into the system for my own self-preservation. I became bitter and angry. My smile came slowly because of my mistrust. I felt betrayed. I walked alone into the woods looking for answers and sometimes I cried. *A Scar Upon Our Voice* is a poetic telling of the latter part of my journey without a path and my coming to understand that a path for me did not exist. I had to create my own. I want the young people to know that only by letting our voices rise and our hearts be heard can we come together and begin to create a path that loves the people.

I want others to know what we experience in our daily lives so it may create a better understanding between us. I want them to know our total dedication and commitment and our divine right to remain who we are and what is meant when we say we will never die. You can take from me what you will but you cannot touch the words of my heart.

I hope as you read this book that you sense the underlying struggle to be free. You have the right to be free but you must fight for that right. You have to struggle to maintain it. Freedom is having a choice based on the truth. I choose to love myself and others. I create purpose and meaning-fulness for myself by building a life around that choice.

A simple gesture born out of kindness is like a single ray of the morning sun piercing the darkness and reaching the sleeping bird and bringing him to song. A simple gesture born out of kindness is like the wind come gently weaving through the voices of the leaves telling me to hope and making me wonder if I have heard the whisper of God. A simple gesture born out of kindness can cause love to suddenly flood from a heart that was once thought to have gone dry. A simple gesture born out of kindness can create a flower never before seen like a rose growing from barren stone. A simple gesture born out of kindness can stitch hope into a torn heart and turn a dying spirit into a gift to the world. A simple gesture born out of kindness may be the only coin that the lost and lonely soul has left to give to another in need. *A Scar Upon Our Voice* is my simple gesture. ⇝

—Robin Coffee
Tahlequah, Oklahoma
2005

Voices
of
the
Heart

(1990)

Introduction

The mother
of
my
words

the undying spirit
of
the People

The father
of
my
words

the
attempt
to
destroy
the
People

Their child
cries
upon the pages

Laughter of Our Children

(published by
Indian University Press, 1983)

Little Indian Boy
Goes to public school
Dies of loneliness
Played
Alone outside
No one
Knew
When he laughed
He cried

Celebrated Columbus day
Don't they know
The price he pays
For the ships
That came ashore

When time came for a student play
Avon lipstick was put upon his face
Plastic feathers on his back
He was told to dance
And
Make it rain

Little Indian boy
Goes to public school
Dies of loneliness
Played alone outside
No one knew
When he laughed
He cried

The old men that know of this
Hang their heads in sadness
The warriors hang theirs in
shame

On a quiet summers day
While all other students have
gone away
Listen
Listen
Quietly

With avon lipstick on his face
And plastic feathers on his back
You can hear him dancing
You can hear him dancing

Then it begins to rain

It begins to rain

Creator
Give us a day
With clouds so black
They turn the day
To twilight
In the moment of silence
Before the storm
Let us throw away
The weeds of hopelessness
Let the rain
Come crashing
Washing
Them away
Give us
A day of rebirth
Let us turn
The crawling infant
Into a walking man
Let his voice
Ring clear
As
The redbird's song
Let the child
Of the spirit
Walk
With all the children
Of
Humankind

Creator
Let us walk
Into
The family
With
Our own voice singing

Voice

He was supposed to go
Wherever it is they go
When they have been destroyed
I
Hear him calling
From the blood
Running through my veins
They thought
They left him
Scattered on the plains
They thought
They left him
Along the trail of tears
They thought
They left him
In prison to rot
He changed
Into the dust
To ride upon the wind
I
Hear him
In courtrooms
In barrooms
On the street
In private homes

He was supposed to go
Wherever it is they go
When they have been destroyed

I hear him calling
From
The blood
From the blood
From the blood

It's early morning
Before dawn
He is alone
He is always alone
He staggers from drink
There is no one left
To believe in him
There will be no pallet
Upon the floor
There is no one left
To care

He lies down
On the cold wet ground

He was once
A mother's son
He was once
A father's hope
He was once
A brother
That fought for brother
And
Little sister

It's early morning
Before dawn
He is alone
There is no one left
To believe in him
There is no one left
To say
Come home

≋

Voices in the Water

We only just met
His name was Buffalohead
We split a bottle of wine
He called it water
To douse
A life's fire
We talked
Of being alone
In the city
Nowhere to go
No one to go to
He was going somewhere
On faith alone he said
I was going somewhere
Alone with my faith
We rode the bus
I could not see his face
Tonight he said
We are
Voices in the water
Strangers in our land
The night became a blur

≋

Loneliness

Loneliness is
The wind without a tree
Lost and wandering
Searching for a reason
Just to be
Loneliness is
Freedom gained
By a single man
To look around and find
He is the only one
Loneliness is
The void of darkness
Between two brightly burning stars
Loneliness is
The heavy burden
Of tears cried alone
In the silence of the night
Loneliness
Rips my soul
Makes my heart walk alone
Loneliness
Shared between two hearts
Is the wind come gently
Weaving through the voices
Of the trees
Telling me to hope
Making me wonder
Have I heard
The whisper of God

Birth

When I awoke
Sunlight broke
A winter's darkness
Born an adversary to the world
I was never meant
To bathe in comfort
To find ultimate happiness
I was born a warrior
A warrior
I will be
Never let the spirit die
The spirit of the People
I will write my words
From blood
On
The
Street
And
Tears
That time cannot dry
The spirit
Flows through my veins
It is
With me
When I walk alone
Born an adversary to the world
Battles lost
And
Won
Scars of life's pain
A spirit
That
Will not die

When I awoke
Sunlight broke
A winter's darkness

The Beauty of Our Lives

When I was young
I
Followed
So many lies
I
Thought I was my enemy
I
Thought I deserved to die
I
Thought I sailed the ocean blue
I
Thought I sailed in 1492
I
Thought Sitting Bull to be so
bad
I
Thought George Washington
was my dad
I
Thought poetry had to rhyme
I
Thought it would given time

Now I know

The beauty of our lives
Does not lie in words
But
In the sharing of our hearts

Our paths have crossed
Our emotions intertwined
A part of each other's lives
We have become

Eternal
Brothers and sisters
In death
We
Will
Not
Part

Raindrop to Rainbow

Leave
A raindrop
On my soul
That I may not forget
A fatherless child
Broken-hearted
Crying alone
So no one would see
So
No one would know
Leave
A raindrop
On my soul
That I might not forget

A mother's youthful face
Disappearing
Into reality
Her
Character
Burned golden
By
Many trials

Leave
A raindrop
On my soul
That I might not forget

The pain
Of being conquered
That
Moment to moment
Brings
Death to my People
Cries
Of anguish
From
Their hearts
Leave
A raindrop
On my soul

When you move
Into
My heart
My Father
That I might change it
Into a rainbow
For all to see

Gift

She was beautiful
In a lost puppy dog
Sort of way
I saw her sitting
On a barstool
Drinking a mug
Of humanity's tears
She smiled
Pages of my life
Turned back
As though
Needing to be re-read
She told
More than asked
You received it too
The Gift
It brought us here together
You thought
No one cared
When I received mine
Angels sang
They
Sang
When you got yours
Life
Let's wait awhile
Before
Returning the Gift
For now
Send a thank-you note
She was beautiful

Something I Lost

All that I remember
There was something
In your eyes
Burned against the sky
Like butterflies

A redbird singing
In your smile
That lit new paths
Across my heart
Like early sun
Upon the morning grass

A gentle breeze
You held
Upon your fingertips
That touched my soul
Like thunder
Leaving my emotions
With gentle rain

A voice
That played
Among the clouds
Like a single
Piercing
Sunbeam

An embrace
That reminds me
Alone in the deserted woods

With strong
And gentle arms
We stopped
A moment in time

All that I remember
There was something
In your eyes
Burned against the sky
Like butterflies

In from the Cold

Warrior

Your journey born
Out of betrayal
You follow the winter path
Barren and cold
Leaving
A trail of loneliness

Warrior

The system rules
And you resist
They tell you to conform
Counselors and confidants
Or
You will surely die

Warrior

You dream of faraway hills
And
Cold streams
The warmth of campfires
And
Morning skies
Nightsongs of beauty
The wind blows
Comfort
Around your spirit

Warrior

The battle is fought
For
The People
Come in
From the cold
Older
And wiser
Take the sharp blade of wisdom
And
Begin a new journey

Freedom

People who are free
Need not live beneath a flag
They do not have dreams
Of freedom

A chained heart
Marks its boundaries
And
Gives its youth
To war

People who are free
Bear hope within their hearts
Like woman heavy with child
They do not find it
In elected voices

People who are free
In giving gifts of love
Cease to exist
Like the river
They flow into
A greater power
Become the universe

People who are free
Wear eyes of compassion
That shed tears
Of great power
To comfort a torn heart
Bring more peace
Than
The rising sun

People who are free
Need not live beneath a flag
They do not have dreams
Of freedom

The Lonely Gifted Traveler

I have walked
The lonely highway
Slept beneath the bridge
Heard the trucks go past
A train whistle blow
Could've died that night
Who would know
I walked a lonely path
Stumbled on a hidden gift

I
Cut
My
Heart

Blood poured
Onto the dust
I formed it into words
Called it
Poetry
≋

I Hear a Drum Calling Me

My heart
Wet with blood
Stretched
Tight with pain
Becomes
A drum
Held by Indian ways
In
A white world
Plays
A song
Beautifully
Tragic
≋

The Eagle's Path

(1991)

Introduction

In the quiet moments of darkness, the stars keep watch.
The night breathes easily. Dream. The rustle of feathers
in the sky. The Eagle comes fierce and warrior-like.

He speaks.

"You began a journey born out of betrayal. Anger and
rebellion filled your heart. You burned like a falling star.
Uncertain and lost, you walked an unknown path and
found the pit of death but would not go in. You sit
in quiet moments of darkness. In your heart clouds gather.
Your soul gasps for life."

The night opens and dawn touches the land.
His last words.

"Follow the Eagle's Path.
Create a life worth all the pain.
Spread your wings.
Claim the sky."

Sevenstars
Lives upstairs with the mold and dust
Drinks cheap wine Night Train Express
Lives with a Canadian Indian
He beats her up drinks her wine
And says he loves her
One daughter drags home men
Rolls them turns cold to them
She has scars around her eyes
She pays her price
One daughter married rich
Comes around at Christmas time
Gave Sevenstars a cup
She put it by her ear
Turns it upside down
It begins to play "Jingle Bells"
She closes her eyes goes somewhere faraway
The daughter raises her blouse
Points her breast at me
And her finger to the couch
The Canadian is passed out on the floor
The summer heat
Coming off the street
Is too much to bear
I know it's time
To head for home
To walk up the cold stream
Disappear into the woods
Build a fire
Spend the night
And think about
Sevenstars
Playing "Jingle Bells"
In the summertime
And looking for something
Deep inside myself
That I have lost

Summer of '74

We had weed
Rolled in our sleeves
And in our hair
And in our dreams

We lived on the dirt roads
And had cold beer
In the back seat
We lived and loved
And fought and became Brothers

We were young and mad
And tough and bad
We were young warriors

In the summer of '74
We lived on dirt roads
And under the old river bridge
We drank and smoked
And wore headbands
And survived

We were young and mad
And tough and bad
And we were young warriors

We had weed
Rolled in our sleeves
And in our hair
And in our dreams

We stayed out for days and nights
We had cold beer
In the backseat

In the summer of '74
That's the way life was
That's the way we were

We survived

No Other Way

I wear scars
Upon my heart
Not
Like medals
Upon my chest
But
Like
A
Warrior
Who
Knows
No
Other
Way
But
To fight

Say This

The world has taken every dream
I ever had
And
Smashed it into the ground

I have watched the years
Fall from my life
Like leaves from an autumn tree

While I lay beat and broken
No one took my hand
Led me from there to here
Alone I have had to walk
Sometimes to crawl
Too many nights I lay and wept
Until I found the strength
To carry on

The world has taken every dream
I ever had
And
Smashed it into the ground

I have watched the years
Fall from my life
Like leaves from an autumn tree

Say this to the world

It was born into my blood
The spirit to fight
The heart
To
Do
It
With

Say this
To
The
World

I still dream

Truce on the Eagle's Path

I will not raise a white flag
A truce . . . maybe
I ran with my youth
On renegade ridge
Drew strength from warriors past
Won some battles
Was told the war is lost
I live
In an agreed upon reality
A system
To bring it about
A truce . . . yes
I will call a truce
You may judge me
As you will judge me
Let the system
Put me where it will
You cannot
Touch
The
Words
Of
My
Heart

My heart declares its freedom
It is brother
To sunrise
To sky
To earth

When life becomes like darkness
My heart whispers to me

New buds on bare limbs
The river flows with strength
No man can stop
The

Sunrise

Touched by a Little Sadness

I know that you must go
Your dream lies somewhere
Faraway

I could tell you
It is in your heart
Like
A sleeping seed
But
I know
You must find it
For yourself

My life is more
Because
Of you
In your going away
It will be less

My heart
Touched by a little sadness

Special and unique
Are words
That come to me
When
Thinking of your smile
And kindness

I walk alone beneath the tree
The leaves struggle in the wind
To break free from the branch
Like
The tears struggling
To break free
From

My heart

My Place beyond Sadness

In special moments
There is a land
I walk

Dip water from the river
Gentle breeze touches me
With woodsmoke
And
Autumn

The sun is setting
The birds and animals
Are not wild
Only
Free
All things are alive
Speak to me

My place beyond sadness

Walking with Crystal

And I remember
When we walked
You were three
We came to some flowers
Purple with yellow
In the middle
At first you wanted
To pick them
But you said
No let's leave them
Someone else may
Want to see them
That would be a good thing
You were this kind of child

Nothing Special

I did believe
My words were
Magical
Mystical
Pure wisdom extract

I have learned
My words are only
Ordinary words
From
An ordinary man

Speaking
From one heart
To another
From me to you

Ordinary words
Like
The ordinary sunrise
Of another day
Like
The ordinary song
Of
The bird

Missing You

I walked along
The old Murrell Home road
In the autumn
I picked the wildflowers
Of goldenrod
And purple thistle
When I thought
No one was watching
I put my hand out
And
Pretended that you took it
We walked together
I talked to you
Told you that I missed you
Told you about flowers
And
Grandma
When it was time to go
I left you with God
To hold you
To keep you
I couldn't see it then
But I can now
How sad I was

It's Not Over Yet

From their paintings
Hanging on the walls
To their poetry
Written in their books
From the slowness
Of their smiles
To
Their everyday struggle
Of
No end

The cries of the lost

They ring from the city jails
They ring from the welfare lines
They ring in the drunks' anger
They ring and shatter reason
From the downcast eyes
Of the children

The cries of the lost

Echo

Echo

From sea to shining sea

Cedar Street Rez

The trailer park reservation
Like a refugee camp
For those abandoned by hope
The irony
Of rain dripping
Through the rusted ceiling
As the utility man
Pulls the meter
"it's cash or no water
no lights. It teaches them
responsibility. Life's hard lessons."

Children of the refugees
Will not live
By the utility man's motto
"The Public Works
for some
but not all"

They wait

For the trumpet's call
Like Eagles on wings
They will fly

Leaving the utility man
With the hard lessons in life
To learn
For
Himself

The Stone Has a Heart

Little Indian boy
Caught grasshoppers
Wondered about clouds
Played ball
Laughed out loud
Went to school
Learned he is brown
Doesn't like to be pushed
And to fight

Little Indian boy
Got a broken family
Became tough
Loneliness came
Brought hunger
Patched jeans
His fist became like rock
His heart like stone
Little Indian boy was gone

Long-haired Indian man
Wandered into the woods
Heard ancient voices sing
"Little Indian boy
little Indian boy
played alone outside

no one knew
when he laughed he cried
little Indian boy
little Indian boy
the stone has a heart
little Indian boy
the stone has a heart
give it a voice
a voice
of chosen words
like
wildflowers
picked as a gift
a voice
of a chosen sunset
a life of beauty
singing into the darkness"

little Indian boy

The stone has a heart

A Whisper of Freedom

Freedom
Will never sing
From shore to shore
It may whisper
From one heart to another

Prayers in solitude
Hand reaching for hand
Turn all else
Into illusion

Possessions
Sought for and chased
Give power to those
That hold them

Those that hold power
Over false freedom
Govern with lies

Freedom

Comes from truth
Prayer in solitude
Hand reaching for hand

It whispers
From one heart to another

Some say
We are born a light
And
Choose the darkness

I say
We are born in darkness
Choose the light

Silently blessed
Beautifully gifted
With life
Spirit of the poet
Existence as an Indian man
My daughter
Silently blessed
Beautifully gifted

I have returned to places
With names
Goats Bluff
Cherokee Landing
Wolf Springs
Welling Bridge
Places of my life
Where any day
You might find me
Writing poems
In my mind
That I plan
To paint across the sky

I am hard sometimes
My heart
Turning in upon itself
I let the world
Make me bitter and angry
My words
Are harsh
Caring little who they hurt
I
Am
At my smallest

I had a dream once
That my words could change the world
But from storm to storm
From disappointment to anger
I clenched my fist
And
Let my dream slip from my hand

My words began to fall from me
Like
Dying leaves
An angry and hopeless voice
Cried silently
Within my heart
In the darkened night
I heard
The heart of the sky
Call out
Through the mournful cries
Of the geese
When one is lost he calls
And
The others answer

I am the lonely voice
Calling

Through the darkened sky
Listening

For the answering call

My heart

Cries out with soft words
That we might find each other
And
Be together
Like
The rain of spring
And
The winter sleeping seed

Sacred Seasons

(1993)

Introduction

Summer
(Fellowship with others)

Come out
From the long shadow
Of evening
Into the sunlight
With tears of sadness
Still upon your face
And the smile
Of your joy
As
We touch

Autumn
(Fellowship with Earth)

Speak to me in your many ways
Of song and beauty
I am your Brother
I will learn your language
You
Touch my heart
To
Teach my mind

Winter
(Fellowship with self)

Look into the reflection of night
With courage and honesty
Do not look away
Break the silence of your heart
With
Blood upon your words

Spring
(Fellowship with God)

I was once a tear you cried
I have the path I followed
Upon your face
Etched
Into my heart

My life
A journey
To find this familiar place

The Dove
(for Crystal)

My heart was on the horizon
A storm without rain
Memories of your laughter
Shattered my quiet loneliness
I could almost bear it
Those times I felt
Your small hands upon my neck
Those times the wind played
This cruel trick on me
No one knows where or when I
cried
I became a passing shadow
Going into the night
I was the rain that would not fall
I was the wind
That would not blow
I was the barren land
I was the cold

My sadness
Is a memory now
Your laughter
Falls around my shoulders
I think of you
As
The Dove

Sent out
To find new land
You found my heart instead
And
Brought it back again
You shattered the depth
Of my emptiness
With
The simpleness of your touch
The way
Sun climbs over trees
And
Rips apart the night

You stood beside me
Took my hand
As
A long awaited rain
Once
Again
Touched the land

39

Older Brother—Fishing

Like
An evening shadow
Upon a rock
You sit unmoving
Silent

You went to Viet Nam
Twenty years later
You came home
You don't talk about it much
I don't ask
The strength of our blood
Cuts through
Years apart and distance

Conversation for the hell of it
We don't need
We are what we are

Like
An evening shadow
Upon a rock
You sit unmoving
Silent

We speak in subtle movements
Natural movements
Of the Earth

The water rolls up gently
To drink
The stone

The day
Goes up in flames
Upon the horizon

We have fought
Different wars
And
Similar ones

We take our peace
Where
We can find it
All I can say

You came home

Poem to Sister
(for Deena)

You suffered
Another defeat in life
Something wanted
You will never have

I saw you
Set your jaw
Bite your lip
You held up
Like
A warrior-lady

In the quiet moments of darkness
You are miles away
The night breeze
Carried to me
The sound of your tears

I love you more
Because of them

Biscuit

Hands moving with the illusion
Of
Living bronze

Shaping a family
Upon
A seasoned board

Like
Ancient elements
Upon
Stone

Etching
The characters
Of
Sons and daughters

Continual movement
Through the years
The hands appear
Like
Dried river beds

Natural monuments
To
Motherhood

She raised seven children alone
Upon
The
Seasoned board

Each one
With
A grateful heart

Beans

Not wanted
By his country

Punished
For speaking
His tongue

His language fell away
Never
Reaching
His sons

White hair and memories

Play like visions
To inward eyes

Seventy years
Have come and gone

Hesitant movements
Announce
His wish to speak

Too-yah

Beans
He says

An old warrior

Looking into the darkness
Finds

His own heart

Too-yah
Beans
I say

And

How do you say
Father

The Mourning Dove's Honor
(for Gina)

I watch the sun
Go
Beautifully
Into the night

Dusk
Was dying
With
Wind blown leaves
And
Passing geese

I think of you
With
The horizon
In my eye

On the crossroads
Of
Your life
You
Chose
Courage and character
Fierce eagles
Guard

Your gentle spirit

From
Your inner strength
You
Create
Such beauty

The mourning dove
Crying
In the evening

Remains silent
In
Honor
As you pass

Dusk
Was dying
With
Wind blown leaves
And
Passing geese

Dream

I see you in the barren landscape
Of the shore
Silver shadows fluid in the moonlight

We hold each other by a single fingertip
Listening to the ancient song
Of water's
Gentle caress upon the stone

The nightbird's gentle glide across the surface

The night makes promises
To our hearts

Your kisses are of slow urgency
Taste
Of
New flowers and of rain

You see the moon reflected
In the single tear
Upon my face

Years of wandering and of seeking

I am drawn to the fire of your soul

You bring my heart to life

One thousand fireflies in the distant grove

A single cloud passing before the moon

Voice of the nightbird calls

Earth turns toward dawn

I see you in the barren landscape
Of the shore
Silver shadows fluid in the moonlight
We hold each other by a single fingertip
Listening to the ancient song
Of water's
Gentle caress upon the stone

The Artists and the Singers

Your voices come to me like an old friend
In the distance
Coming ever closer
Turning into a vision of the early morning sun
Chasing dawn
And
Touching sleeping birds bringing them to song

Artist
You are the mystic dreamer
That speaks your heart in symbolic words
That cross the eternal distance
Between your heart and mine

Singer
You blend your voice and music
To create an unheard voice
That comes into being like the birth of a child
Bringing
Not only beauty but a cleansing
That lifts the veil around my heart
Allowing me
To hear its voice

It is from your courage
To open
This passageway
That I find my strength to speak

We are as different
As the Earth and Rain and Sky
Yet
Together we grow like a strong tree

Each of our hearts a bud bursting open
As our lives
Slowly unfold like new leaves

Creation moves among us

Our different voices become a single sound
Calling others
From
Winter's lonely hands

We become the neverending circle
Of brothers and sisters
Knowing
Each other
By the sound of our hearts

Dream #2

You are distant
Like
A treasured memory

Your absence is like a sadness
And
This sadness a joy

I hear your voice
Above the chaos
That
Seeks to overcome

Your voice is the harmony
Of all voices
That
Seek to create
A
Light
In the vast emptiness

It is your smile
Against
The background of yellow autumn leaves

And
The feel of dying warm breezes
Touched
With the cool veins of seasons changing
That
I am made from

Simple things tell me

There are only those I love
And those that love me
And everything else
Is the chaos
Trying to overcome

The light we lit
While
Passing through
This
Emptiness

Rivers and Teardrops

There is a great distance
Between your heart and mine
Though we are more alike than different

We are both the rain

I am hard-driven in late spring
Reshaping the landscape
For the new dreamers that will come

You fall gently in late summer
Upon the new lover's face
You hide the tears
While the hard lesson
Of stitching hope into a torn heart is learned

You are beauty seeking passion

I am passion seeking beauty

There is a great distance
Between your heart and mine

As rain
We have come to know

Life is not a destination
But
An everlasting journey

We are more alike than different

A raging river and a soft teardrop

We have come to know
Life is change
And
Turmoil

Dreams and hope

Bittersweet

Wind across This Land

My heart is made fertile
By
Years of struggle
And
Lying desolate

Earth speaks to me
In
Quiet
Moments
The voice
Comes

As the moon behind bare limbs
Bringing
Promises of brotherhood
When
I am touched by loneliness

The voice
Comes

As the mourning dove in the evening
Echoing in the deep woods
Bringing
Promises of peace
When
I am bound in my anger

The voice
Comes

As the blue heron's flight
Silent shadow on water's surface
Bringing
Promises of life
When
I am trapped behind words

My heart is made fertile
By
Years of struggle
And
Lying desolate

The voice
Comes
Scattering seeds upon my soul
Like
The wind across this land

Vision
of the
Winter
Sleeping
Seed

(1998)

Introduction

The end of a long journey. The beginning of a new one.

At the age of 15, I came to the time of my own thinking. I began to see that the things that I had been taught were not always the truth. It seemed to me that I had been educated in a way that concluded that my people and their lives had ended and that the idea of a romantic past was accepted but that the only hope left was to prepare myself to join the system and leave my heritage behind. I felt betrayed. I became angry. I rebelled.

The elders around me, those that had accepted the responsibility to teach and guide and advise me, remained silent to this process. I interpreted their silence as agreement to this process and the comforts it brought them as payment enough for their actions. I lost respect for them. Their words fell from their mouths to the ground. I walked over them. I knew they did not have any answers. I began to search for my own path.

I began to search without guidance, without answers, without a direction. I only knew that my heart was telling me that it was the right thing to do. I knew that there had to be a path that would allow me to continue in the vein of blood of my heritage and to always remember the struggles that were endured to maintain ourselves as a people. The path I searched for would be one I was proud of, that gave me self-respect, and would allow others to live with hope. I thought this path would be easily found.

I started the journey without a path and ended up lost. Every path led me into the system that my heart would not let me join. I watched as others went on into their lives, into schools, into jobs, into their families. I learned that if you do not embrace the system it rejects you. I rejected back. I was angry. I was uncertain. I discovered the brotherhood of the lost. We are of like hearts. We believe that our hearts are right but we cannot find the path that we are compelled to follow. We are the warriors of the people, watching them die, and feeling helpless.

Driven by the warrior in my blood to protect and die for the people, I cannot do otherwise. If I cannot find the path that shelters them, if I cannot find the path that feeds them, if I cannot find the path that nourishes them, if I cannot find the path that loves them, I do not deserve to live. I cannot choose to save myself. I will have failed. I am compelled to go into isolation within myself and begin the slow death of shame. It is this death that is offered as a final resistance to a system my heart will not join.

At times I have come out of this slow death to search again. Joining the system in body but not in heart or mind, I thought I had found a way to provide while I searched for an answer. I became an anti-system Indian. I thought I could move on in life taking on responsibilities of family and home. I had made a mistake. The anti-system Indian cannot have those responsibilities. My heart was calling me. It called me out of the system. I was in conflict with my own heart. I thought I could stand against my heart and win. I thought I could compromise my heart and live.

I could not live with a compromised heart. I was trying to live a life without finding the path that I had started out trying to find. I knew I was trying to save myself. I loved my family and my home but I did not love myself. It was not a path anyone needs to follow. I knew it was going to end. My heart had left me. I was filled with emptiness. I had not found the path. I did not know if there was a path. I turned inward. Isolated. Alone without a heart. My family and home gone. I went to the street. I became a noble drunk. My slow death, my final resistance. I walked an endless void where death seemed the only escape—a form of peace.

I had come to a time devoid of hope. A journey started to find a path of self-respect and life was close to ending in shame and death. The shame was that of a warrior that has failed to fulfill the role of taking care of the people. I had failed to find the path that would lead to safety, provision, and nurturance. I had failed and deserved to die. The shame of the warrior leaves no choice but to turn death into an act of resistance. It is saying that there is no place for my people to live with dignity so I will die slowly before you as a statement against your system. It is making the best out of a hopeless situation. I have failed but I will not waste my death. Shamed and hopeless, I try to help to the end.

It is the heritage of my blood that creates this idea. The heritage that exists within cannot be taken away or destroyed. The warrior in my blood is the gift of the survival instinct. I must fulfill the role of a warrior. The instinct is what causes the need to search for a path that will allow the people to live. The path must be found and it is the warrior in the blood that will continue to resist a system that is not nurturing for the growth and continuation of the people. The survival instinct will continue to send warrior after warrior after warrior out to search for the path necessary to live and those that do not find it must make the most of their death. Many try to hide from this fate, they live as anti-system Indians numbing their emptiness with alcohol and drugs. The noble drunk is defiant and drinking to die.

The cries of the lost can be heard in the sorrow that is seen deep in the eyes and the slowness of the smile. I had these cries etched into my face. I could not remember anyone that loved me or anyone I loved ever crying from happiness. I sat upon an empty bucket in the early dawn watching my breath in the cold morning and draining the corner from the empty wine bottle. I heard my daughter call me. It had been almost four years since our separation. In the mystery of ways, I knew she would call and need me. I got up and walked off the street that day and have never gone back.

I began to walk the Circle of Death. I started to search once again only to come to the same crossroads of the system or death. Deciding not to decide, I was on the journey without a path again. I became an anti-system Indian once more and started numbing the emptiness of my compromised heart to survive. The feelings of rejection and rejecting back were in my heart but it felt more like hopeless resignation than anger. The cries of the lost were still on my face. I was determined not to become a noble drunk and fall into the endless void. The patterns of my life keep repeating.

The dream came to me and when it was over I did not know if I had been asleep or awake. I lay in the silence of the night wondering if it had been real. An eagle had come to me and summed up my life in a few words. "You began a journey born out of betrayal. Your heart filled with anger and rebellion. You burned like a falling star. Uncertain and lost you walk an uncertain path. You found the pit of death but would not go in. You sit in quiet moments of darkness. Your soul gasps for life. In your heart clouds gather." His last words to me: "Follow the Eagle's Path. Create a life worth all the pain. Spread your wings and claim the sky." I would struggle with these words for years.

Voices of the Heart, my first self-published book, was the first sign of life from my heart. I think of the belief that my daughter would call as the first day of spring in my life, the dream of the eagle as the faith of this seed, and the book as the first flower blooming. The month that I had the book ready and took it to the store to begin to share it, the call came. It had been three years since I walked off the street. It had been seven years since I had talked to my daughter. It would be one more year before she would come to live with me.

I had begun to create my life. I took the pieces of paper that I had placed my heart upon and put them together and began to share it. I believe this is a gift from God. I believe it is meant to be shared. I continued to do this and self-published two more books of poetry. I was creating my life. I was becoming a poet. I was becoming more hopeful. But, I did not see any change in anyone around me. I was still living as an anti-system Indian. It was still causing a conflict in my heart. I had not found the path that would allow me to spread my wings. I was far from claiming the sky.

I have always sought my answers in solitude. I believe in God. I believe in divine intervention. I believe in dreams. I believe in visions. Words I had read long ago came back to me: "Without a vision the people perish." I could see this in my life. I knew I was on the right path but I did not know where it was going so I did not know what to do. I understood without a vision I would perish. The warrior, my blood, would see to it.

A gift must be shared. A gift cannot be shared for fame or fortune. If fame or fortune does not come with the sharing, the reason for sharing can be taken away. Sharing the gift is the reason in itself. I have been given the freedom to share this gift in whatever way I choose. It is by the authority of no man that gifts come into this world or the effect they will have once they are shared between hearts. I sought no man's permission to seek the gift of a vision. I ask myself, who was with me when I lay upon the cold, frozen ground seeking to die? I asked no one when I was alone in solitude seeking to live.

At times, my answers have come suddenly in stark clarity. At other times, my answers have come slowly, peacefully as I walked along the shores of water or sat quietly among the trees.

I came over the hill. The hawk was upon the rabbit's back. The rabbit would become the hawk. The hawk would touch the sky. The hawk would fall and become the earth. The earth would wash into the river. The river would rise and become a cloud. The cloud would melt and become a seed. The seed would become the grass. The grass would be eaten and become the rabbit. A Circle of Life.

A Circle of Life. A circle with each part having its reasons, its time, its purpose. A Circle of Life like a circle of seasons—the renewal of spring, the growth of summer, the receding of autumn, the long, silent stand of winter. I have watched it many times while sitting among the trees. I have seen my life like the seasons, finding hope, growing, losing sight of hope, becoming empty. The patterns of my life were like the seasons. The slow, peaceful coming of my answer suddenly shifted into piecing clarity.

The people live within seasons. The people have seasons. The people are in the season of their winter. I saw the people within a seed. The seed within the earth. The earth covered with snow. I saw within the seed the people living. In the heart of the seed, the people were strong and vibrant and calling out to others. In the pulp of the seed, the people were tangled together in a mass. At the shell, the people were haggard and walking aimlessly, drinking, and some were twisted as if dead. People were moving from one place to another within the seed. The people are in winter. The people are in a winter sleeping seed. I am in the winter sleeping seed. I have struggled with this for years. I had to find a way to understand it. I placed the vision over my life and it began to make sense.

My journey began in the pulp of the seed. I was a part of the tangled mass. I had started my search for the path that would allow me self-respect and pride and be a service to the people. I had come to the crossroads of joining the system or death. I had tried to walk between these choices. I started the journey without a path. I was rejected for this and I rejected back. It was anger and rebellion of not being understood and the attitude that my experience was unimportant kept my resistance strong. Also, I knew my heart was right. I was in the position of joining the system or suffering the anguish of poverty. I tried to live as an anti-system Indian. I joined the system in body but not in heart or mind. I thought I could live this way. It caused a conflict in my heart. I had compromised my heart. I drank to numb my emptiness. The emptiness became too much and I quit working. I knew the consequences. The consequences of living in poverty seemed small compared to living with an empty heart.

A certain feeling of pride and righteousness comes with this type of resistance. It feels better than the self-loathing that comes from living against your heart. It is this experience that taught me about the warrior in my blood. The warrior in my blood is one part of my heritage that can never be taken away by anyone or anything. The warrior in my blood demands that I find a path that loves the people. If I do not find this path, I must die. It demands that I make my death a defiant statement.

It is the warrior in my blood that started my journey. I knew the paths offered me did not love my people. I knew the paths offered me would end in emptiness. The warrior in my blood is my true heritage. I touch the earth through my mother and my father. They passed the warrior in my blood to me through their blood. The warriors of the past know the warrior in my blood. I feel them whenever I hear about their courageous battles to the death. The same blood makes me a warrior of this time. I am humbled by the true reality of my undying heritage.

I spent my time as a noble drunk. I had failed to find a path for myself or one that would ease the suffering of my people. By trying to live with a compromised heart, I had hurt the ones I loved the most. I had failed. While trying to keep my shame to myself, the only atonement was to make my death a final resistance. The sudden knowing that my daughter would call me and need me can only be attributed to God's promise that I would not be deserted in the time of my greatest need. I knew as I lay upon that cold, frozen ground seeking death that I was not alone.

I have repeated some of these patterns throughout my life. I call this endless searching and not finding the Circle of Death. After searching so many times, death seems like an easy path. I have tried many times to take on responsibilities while going through this pattern and I have hurt many people. I know that I cannot make commitments. I choose not to love again unless I find the path.

The vision had made sense out of all my past craziness. I had lived within the pulp of the seed. I was searching for something more meaningful. I had tried to find answers in other people and other things. I had my heart written down and put away. I was unsatisfied and isolated within myself. I was alive but mostly just existing. It was when I hurt others that I became overwhelmed by a sense of failure and self-loathing. I lost faith in finding the path. I thought death was an answer. It was, at this time, that I moved out of the pulp of the seed and became part of the shell of the seed. I was drinking to die. I saw no way out except for death. My final act was to protect the people with my statement of death.

The Eagle's Path was my crossing over into the heart of the seed. It was the beginning of my journey from death to life. It was the realization that the path I had searched for did not exist. The path I needed had to be created. I had to create my own life. Create a life worth all the pain. The only boundary was my heart's ability to dream.

I began to create. The journey I had started so many years ago to find the path that would give me pride and self-respect while helping others live with hope was now a journey of building that path. The gift of my poetry was unlocked. The path would be a sharing of my heart. I would break open my heart and share the beauty and the pain. It would be a path to inspire others out of hopelessness. It would be a path to comfort other warriors seeking answers in solitude. It would be a path beginning where I stood. A path open to all of any age. A path that loves the people.

The sacrifices I had to make were to walk out of my silence, to leave behind my lost life, and walk alone with my faith. No greater love than to give up your life for another. I gave up my old life for a new life of helping to build up the people with love and not by the tearing down of others. I am free to take the gift God gave to me and take it wherever I want, whenever I want, and to whoever I want. God is love. I am free to carry a message of love. The burden is light and the yoke is easy. To carry a message to someone you love is not a heavy load and to carry the message using a gift from God is a privilege. The insights of God's truth manifesting in my life were awe-inspiring to me.

The vision of the winter sleeping seed full of people living. A seed can only grow the same from which it came. The winter seed struggles through the long, cold season. The hope of the seed is for the season to change. The seed cannot live without the undying faith born of hope of season's change. Beyond winter there is life. The people are a winter sleeping seed. The hope of the people is a time of coming change. The people do not live without an undying faith born of hope of a coming change. Beyond winter there is life.

The winter seed struggles through the bleakest cold and endless snow. The winter seed is nourished from the center of the heart. The secret of life. The heart of the seed grows as the pulp and the shell move into the heart. The seed prepares itself by listening to the urging of the center of the heart. The seed waits patiently for the sound of the warm and gentle rain of spring. The people struggle through the winter of a cold and bleak system. The people are nourished by the center of their heart. The secret of life. The heart of the seed grows large as the people living in the pulp and the shell begin to move into the center of the heart. The people prepare themselves by listening to the secret of life in their hearts. The people wait patiently listening for the Creator's voice coming like a song from the sky.

The Creator provides for the seed. The Creator provides for the people.

I take these thoughts with me as I walk beside the water. I walk with the certainty that a path that loves the people does exist. I walk with the simple faith of a seed. I walk to hear answers. The birds are feeding on new seed. The fish rise to take the fallen insects. The earth is their system. It is ours too. We are in the winter season. The snow or system falling upon us is not our system. It is not ours to join. It is a field to be harvested. A field to provide what is needed by the seed to stay alive. The falling snow cannot touch the undying faith born of hope of season's change. Our faith is the struggle to maintain ourselves as a people. The struggle is born into our blood.

I am born a warrior of this time. I do not have to drink to die. My death does not have to be my statement. My life will be my statement— a form of peace.

I have followed the eagle's path into the heart of the seed. I have sacrificed my fears and lost life. I have turned the system into a field of harvest. I looked into my vision and chose my dream. I am the struggle that keeps the seed alive. I walk to this dream by sharing my gift. I have found a path that loves the people. I wait patiently for a time of season's change. I listen for the sound of a warm and gentle rain falling through the leaves like a song from the sky. ▱

Song of the Sky

The final aching rays of autumn
Have touched me
Falling dream-like
I am surrounded by earth
And a strange stillness
Bitter wind blows overhead
Brittle limbs are rattled
The long winter season
Has come to my life
Wrapped in the tattered layers
Of my memories
Of lost journeys
And broken dreams
I shiver in the loneliness
Of my cold
While the moon burns bright
The stars clear
I make no noise
Against the night

To a cold and frozen earth
Comes a warm and giving rain
To the winter sleeping seed
Still clinging to its faith

Comes
The song of the sky

The Creator wrote this song

I am brought to life
By
The beauty of its sound

Together
We change the season

Change the earth

From
Death to life

Searching

There is a sacred echoing
In my blood
It is the echo
Of
A warrior's birth

Crossroads

I stood alone
Beside still water

Shadows of dark
Jagged and long

I knelt down
Whispered
My voice

Rippling the surface

Casting

My insignificant light
Into
The darkness

Children of Tomorrow

Children of tomorrow

Their tears will not fall
In the tracks
Of our sorrow
Be willing to give up life
That others might live

That is my heritage

I say
To the trees and clouds and sky
That is my heritage
Forever

Prayer

With a gentle hand
Comfort me
Give me strength
To walk
In my own

Silent resistance

Endless Void

When living seems wrong
And
Dying right
It's like walking dead
Into
An endless night

Left with the choice
To join
This system
Or
Suffer in shame

Which way is right
Which way is right

I walk dead
Into an endless night
Living seems wrong

Dying
So
Right

Compromised Heart

I am quiet tonight and alone
I look at the pictures
Of
Grandparents
Parents
Brothers
Sisters
Child
Myself
Flowing throughout the images
A strong
Sense of pride
I feel their blood
Still living in mine
I feel the strength
Only family can give
I feel the eternal bond
Of shared tribulation
We are strong
In
Pride
Blood
And
Struggle
I know the pain I have endured
Is no more than theirs
We are bound together
In our struggle
To maintain ourselves
As a people
We do not understand
The merciless need of others
To take this away
The desire to do so
Cannot come
From a God of eternal love
We know our hearts are right
We will fight for this right
Forever

Suffer endlessly
Anything less
Is to cease to exist
We know the struggle of one another
Having lost
Within a generation
Language
Traditions
But
The words of our hearts
Cannot be touched
Resistance born of anger
Will not allow
My heart
To walk into a system
That promises no hope
Resistance is a path I followed
Never finding life
Seeing death approach
I turned inward upon myself
Drinking myself into nothingness
Afraid to die
No reason to live
I compromised my heart
Just to survive
I survived
Just to exist
I remained silent
Fighting the conflict
Of the heart
Being torn into emptiness
A compromised heart
Living against itself
Dousing
Its life fire

I could not look
Into
My own eyes
Too
Much truth
For me to bear

Alone
Lonely
Angry
And
Ashamed

I saw a redbird

In the highest branches

Of a barren winter tree

And

Wondered

When my heart

Would fly

Away from me

Anti-System Indian

Compromise is a betrayal
Killer of spirit

A conflict of the heart

Walking the path of the system

Takes me away

From who I am

It takes strong drink

To numb the spirit

Of a heart

That wants to live

But cannot find a reason why

Sleepless nights of anger

Searching desperately

Never finding

The voice of the lost

Falls silent

Moans of anguish

Echo in the empty heart

I join

The circle of Brothers lost

Death comes squirming

Like a pup on its belly

Embracing death

While it pisses on me

Is the only freedom

I have known

Sacrifice of Our Silence

I ask forgiveness from you
My mother
For telling this

Striking me
Not from anger I understand
But from an inconceivable grief
Of a mother alone
With hungry children

Put salt on paper
To quiet my hunger

I know you could not give in
Or give up
Despair
Is the luxury of the lonely
And
You had us

I can understand much more
How your home
Is your heart
At times
You fed my friends
My family

Memories
Echo strongly

It is as a grown man
I go back
And put my arms around you
You run
On the path
Between my heart and mind
My heart cries
My hand
Only

Sheds the tears

We do not belong to this world
And never will

Not because we are so wounded
But
Because we are so beautiful
And
Cannot find a place to grow
Your incredible strength and love
Are the greatest gifts
They still carry me
Through the darkness

I put salt on paper
To quiet my hunger

You changed the salt to words
And
Quieted my hungry heart

I ask your forgiveness
My
Mother
For telling this

It is the way you have taught

I hear the cries of hungry children
They need your strength
And love

⇒

Faith Is a Struggle

Undying faith
Of the undying seed
Cannot be touched
By the long cold winter

Words of my heart
Cannot be touched
By the long cold winter

Faith is the struggle
Of the undying seed

Words of my heart
Are the struggle

Of the winter sleeping seed

I am the struggle

I am the struggle

I am the struggle spoken

Warrior-Child
(for Amanda)

Warrior-child
Born out of betrayal
And
Of
Pain

Anger takes
The voice of your heart
Your vision to remain

Warrior-child
I open my heart to you
I offer this hauntingly quiet place
Hope that you find comfort
And
Cry within my silence
Gentle
Tears
That stand against the night

Warrior-child

I want to be the eagle
Tear raw flesh from bone
To feed the young
Watch until you have grown
Move aside
As you listen
To the sound
Of your own voice
Scream against the wind

Warrior-child

You are morning rain
Falling into dreams
You bring flowers
From

Stone
You are morning tears
Faraway
Cried alone

You break my heart open
Good-bye
Is the hardest
Part of you

Warrior-child

Born out of betrayal
And
Of
Pain

Anger takes
The voice of your heart
Your vision to remain

Warrior-child

Turn

Let words of hope

Be the way
That we are strong

Pale purple petals touched with
yellow
You bore the weight of winter
And
Cast your gentleness

Against the world

⇒

Warriors of This Time

I do not see the enemy
I see the people dying
I do not see the wounds
I hear the wounded crying

Warriors of this time

I do not know
Where your battles lie

But

I hear the wounded crying
I see the people dying

Seasons of Our Lives
(for Crystal)

You came back to me
Broke
The winter death of my life

The early season redbud
With leaf
Slowly unfolding
Our hearts
Became
Like that

I watched you struggle
And grow
A quietness came between us

Autumn in our blood

We grew apart

Seeds fall to earth
Love will have its way
When you carry seasons in your
heart

I grow happy and sad
Thinking of our winter
As
Distance apart

We will remain strong
With
The scent of redbud blossoms
Flowing
In
The
Blood
Of our hearts

Warriors Slay the Predator

Night with an empty sky
Screams of broken hearts
Fall to the ground
Dying
Without a sound

No place to turn
No place to go
Life and death seem the same

Pain
Whispers without sound
Teaching
What I do not want to know
The
Meaning
Of
Alone

The world is a predator
Killing
And
Wounding hearts
Making
Death seem like a form of peace

Warriors slay the predator
Those not slain
Will
Slay the children

Warriors
You will not be alone
With your hearts torn
But
Unwilling to die
You
Will hear whispers of hope
Coming
Like the hands
Of
God
Unfolding
From
These gentle unfolding hands
Comes
A newborn's cry

Beautifully killing death

Chant of Life

Every day I live
Is another day
I die

I have known this
When first
My eyes touched sky

I began my chant
To
Sing against my death

I began my chant
Breathing
Young child breath

The rain never ceases
In its fall
The river never ceases
In its flow

Kindness born of love
Kindles
The dying soul

The rain and the river
Touch beauty to my eye

Kindness born of love
Turns
The moments until I die

Into

Life

So desperately beautiful
≋

A Heart Moved

Some say spring
Is
The most beautiful

The time of living

New life

Promises of hope

I have watched the dying
And
Through it

Have come to know

The depth of my love

And

Because of that

Have become more loving

Of

The living
≋

The Eagle and the Cross

(2000)

Introduction

In the startling clearness of daylight, I read the writing I have done at night.
I realize that as I go further into the deepness of the night that I shed
layer after layer of my daily life. I reach the layers of my own desires
and selfish longings (greed, power, etc.).
When I write at these levels, my words do not have much impact on me.
It is only when I go into the very depths of the night and shed all my
layers that my words are meaningful to me in the daylight.
It is only when I can touch the surface of my heart and feel the seeping
blood, see it upon my finger, taste it, do I know I am at the level to write.
I have been given the gift of experiencing this life as an American Indian
man, facing the present situations, and in my present surroundings.
God is masterful in this plan. Wise and beautiful.
The only way to insure eternal perfection with a child such as I,
is with forgiveness.
Perfection could not exist without forgiveness. The cross was not an
afterthought in the creation process.
Wherever people have existed, they have created symbols of their beliefs
and values (i.e., the Cross).
I have adopted the eagle as a symbol in my life.
When I see an eagle, it holds me in wonder of the power of the heart
that could create such a majestic being.
I see in the eagle beauty, grace, fierceness, strength, mystery, power,
while knowing of the eagles' gentleness with their young.
The eagle follows a different path everyday and completes a circle
in the evening.
The eagle is a symbol of all life on this planet, including the earth.
The eagle comes and grasps my heart with strong talons and flies
beyond the sky
to release my heart. All of life cries out my words to the blood on the cross.
God hears my heart and bread begins to fall from heaven like manna
from the sky. The two paths I follow to life—The Eagle and the Cross.

The Eagle and the Cross

Our lives are a reflection
Of the spiritual truth
God watches over the universe
Eagle watches over the earth
Eagle flies free and beautiful
A symbol of the truth

God's shadow

The eagle touches the sky
I touch the earth
It is our distance apart
That gives birth
To the yearning in my heart
I long to soar upon his wing
But I cannot
Eagle dives from the sky
For us to be together
There must be death
The sacrifice of life
The Eagle and the cross
≂

The Blood of a Warrior

Through my veins
Old blood runs
Alive having survived
Many battlegrounds
It raises its voice
Against
The illusion of freedom
In a promised land
It raises its voice
Against injustice for all
Amber waves of pain
The voice of warrior-blood
Stirs my heart
To rise and stand
Like
30 warriors
Against
200 cavalrymen
≂

Shattered Silence

A silence exists
Created by the void
Of our unspoken hearts
I will raise
My voice
In this silence
Like dropping a little stone
To gauge
An unknown depth
Many voices
Of little stones
Fill the silence
Bring death
To empty echoes
Of the void
The silence waits
For stories
Struggles of the heart
Tribulation of the people
The courage
Of the old ones
That stood
And faced
This life
Day by day
⇒

Within Her Eyes
(for Lidia)

Eyes that draw attention
Like a beautiful oddity
In a starry sky
Mystery upon mystery
A lifetime of searching
Could not unravel
Conflicting emotions
Brought into alliance
By gentleness
Demanding respect
A powerful shyness
Softly voicing
Imprisonment
Of a beautiful heart
A heart
That will not be silenced
It speaks
From
Within her eyes
⇒

Walk with Me

There is yet time
To walk with me
Down a path
Between the trees
We can talk
About how the world
Is just a chisel
In the hand of God
Chipping us free
Into children of deep joy
Walking home
We can talk about
How sometimes
I think God
Is not indifferent
But more like
A father
Pretending to watch tv
But worries
Until
In the distance
Floats the laughter
Of children coming home
⇌

Gravediggers Be Warned

The skeleton of earth
Juts out
With the bones
Of my people
Hills and mountains
There is no need
To dig
In sacred soil
Listen to the hills
Listen to the mountains
You will learn
Who we are
You might find
Your true self
Being carbon-dated
And under
The microscope of God
⇌

The Spirit of Struggle

Struggle burns on the inside
With flames of courage
Eyes of fire
Burn away the night
Struggle lives in the heart
When flickering low
Prays for winds of hope
To restore its light
Struggle when dying into embers
Like morning ash
Circled in stone
Waits in the still dawn
Struggle listens for the wind
Or the voice
Of just one
To touch his heart
Making him cry out
In warriors' song

Warriors' Song

They rode their stallions
Courageously into the sky
Truth burned deep within
The look of their eyes
They sang the song of warriors
We will never die

They rode their stallions
Courageously into the sky
Truth burned deep within
The look of their eyes
They sang the song of warriors
We will never die

They rode their stallions
Courageously into the sky
Truth burned deep within
The look of their eyes
They sang the song of warriors
We will never die

They rode their stallions
Courageously into the sky
Truth burned deep within
The look of their eyes
They sang the song of warriors
We will never die

Better to Give Than Receive

Silent and still we can lie
Until our hearts beat together

I am battle weary
In this war of life
Too many wounds
And too much strife
Lay down beside me
Place your soft heart
Against my back

Silent and still we can lie
Until our hearts beat together

You are not fragile
But your heart seems so thin
Mine is scar-tissued
And so toughened
Your softness takes away
Some aches and some pains
I know it is compassion
That brings you here again

Silent and still we can lie
Until our hearts beat together

I am touched by the soft way
You breathe upon me
The way you say I am
A warrior far from home
To comfort me is a pleasure
To suspend the world
While you remove my pain

Silent and still we can lie
Until our hearts beat together

You see this world
For what it is

Important things that others miss
We share silence
Like others share a kiss
You encourage me
To pursue my dream
You are much too worthy
Of me it seems
But you say no

Silent and still we can lie
Until our hearts beat together

You say I am a gift to you
You are more a gift to me
You are the difference
Between sane and insanity
You say I am a warrior
Fighting to keep a vision alive
Battling on a rocky slope
Where no lonely heart can thrive
You are more than comfort
You are compassion come alive

Silent and still we can lie
Until our hearts beat together

We are old souls come together
We find beauty in the struggle
We have always been here
And we always will be
I think that is true
As long as others care
The way you care for me
And me for you

Silent and still we can lie
Until our hearts beat together

My words are only
The disarray
Of where I have been
My path
Is like the wind
Where I am
What I am
Is
Searching on
≈

Simply Changing the World

Reaching out
A single hand
Like a single drop
Of warm rain
On winter's pain
Falling on crying souls
And caressing
The lonely places
We share
Reaching
So very close
To
The meaning of love
≈

We Are All Words

Life comes
After love
Flowing
From the mouth
Of the living word
Like a stream
An ocean
A whisper
A shout
Someday
We will discover
We are all words
To the same song
Echoing
Through the universe
On the voice
Of God
≈

The Path of Hope

Rainbows come
After the storms
Like hope
After
Tribulation
≈

Voice of the System
(for Calvin)

They have all become
Voices of the system
The ones
We once knew
Turned their backs
On the greater good
The higher goal
Of true freedom
Brush them from our boots
Like dust
From an unfriendly city
Let us go back
The three springs
See if we can stand
To look
Into our own reflections
Or
Let's gather the turtle shells
Aged
For the love potion
The one
Someone steals each time
Right before they're ready
Or

We can shoot some squirrels
The kind without tails
You remember
The one you didn't
Give me
Or
We could just sit
And remember
How we used to sneak
Through town
The car wasn't legal
Neither
Was our condition
Or
Talk about today
We have not become
Voices of the system
We still believe
In the greater good
The higher goal
True freedom for our people

In brotherhood
More power to you

Shadow of Death

A spirit alone
Rips itself away
From flesh and bone

There is a place of living
Apart from life
Many are the blessed
That do not know
This endless void
Many are the blessed
Having had to walk
Through it
The valley of the
Shadow of death

A spirit alone
Rips itself away
From flesh and bone

Crystal

If all the birds
Of the world
Sang at once
This coming dawn
It would not come close
To the beauty
Of the first sounds
You made
When I held you
Only hours old
Whatever pain
I find
On my path
Through this existence
I can endure
Without bitterness
Or anger
Because
I have been paid
By God
With the gift
Of you

To Touch the Wind

The founding fathers
Set into motion
Through acts of legislation
The method of my death
A slow beating

To keep the noise down
To hide the blood
To prevent outrage
To slowly beat
The Indian
Out of the man

The slow beating
Moaning through history
The cries of torn culture
The ripping out of tongue
Stomping on traditions
Tribalism
Ridicule of religion
Spiritual beliefs
The sound of ripping flesh
As the generations
Were pulled apart

The slow beating
From childhood to grave
Surrounded at school
Called a dirty Indian
Watching as
Kansas wheat-farm boys
Became caricatures
Of Indian stereotypes
Mothers and fathers
Lost
Drunk
Missing in action
Adapt or die
They were dying
Without hope
Dignity
Identity
Answers
Each other

Dying in silence
Without hope
No answers
For their children
Without hope
Despair
Choosing alcoholism
Over
Hopelessness
Creating a new circle
One
Of death

Segregation
Indian reservation
Assimilation
Boarding school education
Relocation
Scattered population
Termination
Defiles creation

The slow beating
From generations past
Cripple me
I cannot get up
My life seems powerless
Like a feather
Caught in a storm
The effort of my life
Seems
An almost silent
Muffled cry
Against
Past and present pain
In our children's eyes
Will
They be
The generation
To finally die

I have walked
The downward spiral
In the
Circle of death

But
I have chosen
To walk out again
That
I might create
An
Image in words
That exposes
What
A slow beating
Will do
To a nation of people
Of what
It has done to me

To create
An image in words
Of
A smoldering resistance
Waiting
To be touched
By
A new wind
Bursting
Into a revolution
Created
By mothers and fathers
Tired
Of
Watching
Their children die

To create
An image in words
Of
My heart

At least
To touch the wind
That will blow
Through the window
Of a child

In summer darkness
Giving them understanding
That in this world
They cannot afford
To love their ass
More than their heart
That their only weapon
Against
The slow beating
Might be
The words of their heart
Muted
From their voice
By silent rage

In the desperate moments
Between
Being lost forever
Or
Becoming a warrior
They will deny
Their
Precious pride
Choose
To stand
Cut their heart
Smear angry blood
Across their words
As they fall
Into the darkness
Of
Their own generation
They
Will find
Their voice
Use the only weapon
They have
At least
To touch the wind
That will blow
Through the window
Of a child
In summer darkness

The Sounds of Morning Coming

The sounds
Of morning coming
Are heard within
The hearts
Of our respected Old Ones
For
They carry the vision
Born in the moments
Of grief and rage
When
Their Warrior-Fathers
Died in the battle
Between
Our extermination
And
Our right
To remain
A People

The respected Old Ones
Carry
The vision
Of
First to endure
Then
To survive
Finally
To rise

Through ceremony
They name the children
In hope
That this one
Will be a warrior
That
Finds
Dying for the People
Too easy

That understands
Living for the People
Is the measure
Of the courage
Of
Their
Hearts

A new warrior
To carry
The vision
Of the Old Ones
For
They have endured
They have survived
The vision waits
For any heart
To
Test itself

Are you strong enough
To
Rise
And
Join the circle
Of
Your own blood
To sing
Your own song
Are you strong enough
To embrace
All the colors
Of creation
To be whole and complete
To be generous
And
Compassionate

Are you strong enough
To live
For your people
To take your gifts
And
Personal strengths
Wield them
As a knife
Cut
Through the blanket
Of silence
Placed over our past
To deny us
Our future
Are you brave enough
To measure
Your life
Against
This
Vision

The
Sounds
Of
Morning
Coming
Are heard
Within
The
Hearts
Of
The respected Old Ones
And
Between
The sound
Of
Morning coming

And
The song of the bird

They sit

In silent anticipation

Listening

For
The
Cry
Of

A willing heart

Rising

To
Meet
The
Vision

Existential
Warrior

(2003)

Introduction

The trials of life have taught that patience is necessary when confronted by situations and circumstances that are not within the individual's ability to change. The patience to endure exposes the transitory nature of crisis and reveals the potential for adaptation and the ability to reason creatively. The process builds confidence and character through experience. The accumulation of experience increases patience and reduces the uncertainty of one's ability to handle crisis. Confident of one's abilities, aware of the potential that exists within, there is the birth of an idea that a life can be created and lived that makes all the trials worthwhile. This idea is called Hope.

Existential Warrior is one of the adaptations that have come out of this type of situation. Captured in the endless void, where death seems the only escape, I have created my own path—a path that leads into the life of a poet with the undying Hope that one day we will all be free and at peace with ourselves and others.

We can always have Hope.

The Blood Part I

It is the story
Of
Our
Blood
That
Intertwines
Our
Destinies

Voice of our blood
We
Recognize
To
Know
Brother
And
Sister

Emotion of our blood
We
Feel
And
Call

Cherokee

The path
Of our blood
Through
The
Veins
Of time
Is
Our story

We are the children
Of this
Story

We are gathered
In the heart
Of a seed
Waiting
On the
Edge
Of
Seasons
Change
Listening
For
The
Voice of God
To
Come
Like
The first warm rain
Bursting
Forth
Like redbud blooms
In
Early
Spring

The children of hope

Born
From
The
Prayers
Of
Our
People
≈

The Blood Part III

The journey of our blood
Like
The journey of rain
Uncertain
Unknown
But
Where we started
And
Where we end
Is
The heart of God
Our
Home

We flowed there
once
As a peaceful stream
Were
Cried
Upon
This
Land
Like
Gentle
Rain

Our lives
Have
Become
The
Struggle
To
Return
Following
The
Sacred
Echoing
Of
God's voice
In
Our
Blood

Whispering our name

Cherokee

Cherokee

Cherokee

The Lesson of Life
Taught by a Hard World

There is only
Those you love
And
Those that love you
Everything else
Is the chaos
Trying
To put out
The
Light
You
Lit
While
Passing
Through
This
Emptiness

Winter
Will come
Many
Will die
Some
Will sleep
As
Seeds
The gentle rain
Of
God's voice
Will
Fall
Upon the seeds
And
A nation will
Arise
From
Their
Hearts
Battle-weary warriors
And
Warrior-ladies
Take
Hope
In the truth
Teach
That
That it might
Be
Taught
The land is barren
And
The seeds too few
Find
Your path
In this task

The seasons
Are
Not ours
To change
Watch
The
Earth
The gentle rain
Of
God's voice
Will Whisper
To
Your heart

Creation
Of
The
Final nation
Separate
The wheat
From
The chaff
From
This
Struggle
Comes all beauty

Souls
Crying out
From
Lost paths
With
Song

Artist
Creating
A
Path

With
Color

Existential
Warriors
Dreaming
Dreams
Of
Hope
That
Will
Never
Die

The
Creation
Of
The
Final nation
Truth is
The
Only
Water
For
A
Heart
Gone
Dry

The
Gentle
Rain
Of
God's
Voice
Touches
The
Seed

Winter
Passes away
Our
Strength
No
Longer
The
Weapons
In
Our
Possession

Our
Strength
Measured
By
The
Nation
We
Build
From the beauty
Of
Our
Hearts
For
The
Children
We
Love
Today

Innocent Sadness
*(for the Ladies at Eddie Warrior
Correctional Center for Women)*

She stood
At the prison gate
No more
Than 7 or 8
Auburn hair
With
A thousand yard stare
Autobiography
Of
Despair

Hurting so long
For nothing
Done wrong
But
To love someone

Dare
Not
To
Smile
Sometimes
After
Awhile
Mommy
Don't come

Little girl

You gotta understand
It's called justice
In our
Great
Land

Just
Deal
With it

More
Or
Less

We
Got
No
Answer
For
Innocent
Sadness

⇝

The Brotherhood Is
Understood

I have watched
Their eyes
For
Too long
Sad
Like
A people
Without
A song
Of their own

Reflection
In
The
Rearview mirror
My
Eyes
Have
Become
The
Same

Jumpstart
My car
Drive fast
To
Outrun
The
Smoke
Old Indian
Doing
The same
Passes me
Going
The other
Way

We wave
And
Grin

The
Brotherhood
Is
Understood

Honor the Old

He was old
But
Not
Feeble
Stiff
But
Not
Unbending

The bayonet
Went
In the
Front
And out
The
Back
Lifted
Off his feet
And
Thrown
Aside
But
His
Daughter
And
Grandbaby
Had
Time
To slip
Away

Honor
The
Old

They
Are
Brave
In
Unimaginable
Ways
⇌

Old One—Your Voice Stirs Cherokee Spirits

Silent
Your voice
Passes
Like
The
Wind
Through
The
Trees
And
Is
Gone

Rising

Your voice
Stirs
Cherokee
Spirits
Like
Leaves
On the wind

Dancing beautifully

Before

Dawn
⇌

Cherokee Dad

Old Cherokee Dad
Pants
A little too high
But
Ready to fight

Son-in-law
No good
Beat the daughter

Cherokee Dad
Intervened
Got
Beat
To
Death

Son-in-law
Sent
To
Prison
For
Life

Daughter
No longer
Lives
In
Fear

Sadness maybe

But

With
The meaning
Of
True
Love
That
She
Will
Give
To
Her
Son

Teachings of the Old Ones

Create with your mind
Guide it with your heart

To
Create
Only
For
Riches
With
The hope
Of
Buying
Freedom
Is
The
Oppression
Of
Your spirit

Create
To
Ease
Suffering
Great or small
Be
Driven
By
Compassion

Give yourself to this
And
You
Are
Free
Your hope
Will
Exist
In a world
Of
Giving
And
Compassion
The
Last
Will
Become the first
The way
God
Says
It will be

⇒

Dawn
Kills night
Like
Memories of you
Ease
The pain
Of
My troubled heart

Moments
It seems
Were
All we had
In your going
You
Taught me
The preciousness
Of
Time
And life

How beautiful
God's concept of family

Dawn
Kills night
The way
You
Remove darkness
From
My
Heart

Whitebird Creates a Poet

I saw a whitebird
Big
Like no other
Ran home
Mom said
Grandpa said
When you see
A big whitebird
It will be me
And so
We knew
He died
He had come
To tell
Her good-bye
And
To break me free
From
This world

I talk
To the plants
And
The birds
Naturally
As I talk to you
This
World
Comes
Hard
After me
The harder it comes
The
More
Beautiful
I become

And

That is how

Whitebird

Created a poet

(for Summer Dawn)

I would rather see you
Free
Even if it is
Walking away from me

I would rather see you
Free
Even if it is
Walking away from me

My arms
Not long enough
Not strong enough
To reach you
Through the concrete and steel
But
My heart is free
To cross any distance
Between us
I want to caress and whisper
To your heart
The secrets I have been told
By living hard
Lying drunk beside
A dark and lonely road

The world is a prison
We are all prisoners
With different privileges

To love
To be loved
Is the only freedom
We will ever know

Love
Or allow yourself
To be loved

I would rather see you
Free
Even if it is
Walking away from me

I would rather see you
Free
Even if it is
Walking away from me

Old Warrior-Lady

Her spirit
Reflects
On her eyes
Like
Sunlight
Shattered
On water's surface
Like
Sunrise
Splintered
Through
Morning trees
Like
Sunset
Dancing
Beautifully
Before death
Old Warrior-Lady
Reaching
For my hand
Makes
Me stand
Give
Voice
To
Hearts
Without
Tongue

When I Am Gone

When I am gone
I hope they say
His mother
Taught him well

If there were
Such a thing
She would be named
To the All-Indian team

Raised seven kids alone
Worked herself
Till bone
Rubbed on bone

There are laws
Written on her heart
Greater than man
Could ever write

How lost I was
Years of wandering
She never quit being mom
To me or any child she met

She doesn't have her language
Ceremonies or traditions
She is Indian the Indian way
She is Indian in her heart

She is a leader
Of the greatest kind
She leads
By being herself

She is content
Being the quiet foundation
On which the people
Can stand and arise

When I am gone
I hope they say
His
Mother
Taught him well

Must Never Forget

Now the hurt
That comes to me
I must feel

I have given up
The hiding place
Of
Sweet nothingness

I must find the way
To make peace
Turn
Walk away

Must never forget
But
I must forgive

Gain that knowledge
To learn
The ways of wisdom

Lay down the weapons
Of
Death
Take
Up the weapons
Of
Life

The Pistol or the Poem

I am the conscience of this
nation
Pushed way down low
The deep dark secret
Never to be told
I am hunted down
By
Rewritten history in the books
State governments smell my
blood
Like
It is gold
I am hunted down
Pushed into the intersection of
life
Where I sense I am in
The crosshairs of a rifle scope
When I was young I could run
Avoid the decision to become a
man
Now
There are children

Who will teach
If all the angry warriors take up
the pistol
Die as martyrs
In the middle of the street
Tearing someone down
Does not make me a bigger man
Only equal to that
Which
I could not stand

I chose the poem
Over the pistol

To carry my heart
As a cloud
My words
Like spoken raindrops
Of
Hope
Falling
On the barren landscape
Reaching
For any seeds of life

A Scar Upon Our Voice
(for my Mother)

We have never spoken
To each other
In our Native Tongue
We speak
A foreign language
Like
A scar upon our voice

The folly of men
Through legislation
Empowered cavalrymen
To ride
Across this dusty land
Raise their sabers
Against our tongue
But
You have taught me
Another way to speak

Redbuds bloom in early spring
A butterfly above the trees
Caught in the wind
Struggles to get free
One of the most beautiful things
I have ever seen

We have never spoken
To each other
In our Native Tongue
We speak
A foreign language
Like
A scar upon our voice

There is much power
In you
Old Indian woman
With your cane
Like
Mother Earth leaning on
Her faith
Through the winter
For the promised rain

Your flame
Has been my guide
Through all the darkness
Your truth
The glowing ember
You placed into my heart
Knowing
It would kill me
Or
Make me strong
Knowing
You would have to watch
My struggle
Through the pain
Like a butterfly
Caught in the wind
Powerless
Voiceless
Without direction
You sent
Your naked son
On a journey
Where
Boys die
And only
Warriors return

With patience of years
You have watched
Your body bows
To time
And
God's deserved respect
Still
Your spirit stands
Strong like your Father's
Bodark bow
Too strong to be bent
By life's daily strings
You have shown me
That I might understand
You were raising me
From a boy
To a man
We have never spoken
To each other
In our Native Tongue
We speak
A foreign language
Like
A scar upon our voice

Every time we speak
We hear this battle wound
Our words
Have blood upon them
So we cherish
The silence between us
The world howls
Its coldness
Around us

The glowing ember
Of your truth
Now burns
Warm and deep
Within my heart
You have taught me
To speak
In another voice

Redbuds bloom in early spring
A butterfly above the trees
Caught in the wind
Spreads its wings
Of power and beauty
Flies to freedom
Like
A grateful warrior
Once a boy
Now a man
Always
Your
Son
⇒

The Call of God

Stumbling
With
Slacked-jawed, twisted face
Racing against blackness

I
Find him lifeless-like
On my front porch
Covered
In his own warm blanket
Of
Vomit and piss

Are the comforts
Of my life
Enough
For me to ignore the suffering
Of
My brothers

I tie my hair back
Paint my face
Take my weapons
Of
Sharpened pencil
And
Empty page

Warrior-Poet

Prepare to go to war

Once more